Spy School

Written by Jill Eggleton

Illustrated by Trevor Pye

The people in the book

The spy teacher

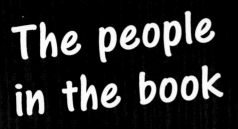

The spy

The place
in the book

The park

The spy teacher was at the park with the spy.

"You have to look for messages," she said. "There are five messages in this park. Go and look for them."

Where will the spy look for the messages?

The spy saw a dog under a tree.

"A message is on the dog," said the spy.

He looked at the dog and saw a message.

This dog has a wet nose!

"Here's a message," said the spy.

"Good," said the teacher. "You have one message!"

Who put the message
on the dog?

A vet?

A spy?

The spy saw a wall.

"A message is in the wall," said the spy.

The spy looked inside the wall.
There was a message.

The man under the tree is a spy!

"Here's a message," said the spy.

"Good," said the teacher.
"You have two messages!"

The spy saw a bottle.

"A message is in the bottle," said the spy.

He looked in the bottle and saw a message.

Look under the seat.

"Here's a message," said the spy.

"Good," said the teacher.
"You have three messages."

The spy looked under the seat.

"A message is under the seat," said the spy.

And it was.
Yuck!
It was a very smelly message.

A skunk was under this seat.

"**Poof**," said the spy. "I have a message."

"**Good**," said the spy teacher. "You have four messages. You have one message to get."

The spy looked all over the park.

"I have one message to get," he said.
"Where is that message?"

The spy looked under the log.
No message.

He looked under the rock.
No message.

Where will the spy look now?

The spy looked under the trees and in the trees.
No message!

He looked in the bins and
under the bins.
No message!

The spy looked in the flowers and under the flowers.
No message!

The spy looked in the duck pond and under the duck.
No message!

The spy looked at the spy teacher.
He looked and he looked.

"A message is under your hat," he said.
"Take off your hat."

The spy teacher took off her hat.
A message was
on her head.

You are
a good spy!

The spy laughed.

"I am a good spy," he said.
"A very, very good spy."

The End

Which are the right messages?

The bird has
a ring on its leg.

Yes? No?

The bird has
a ring on its beak.

Yes? No?

A cat is
in the log.

Yes? No?

A mouse is
in the log.

Yes? No?

A bag is
under the seat.

Yes? No?

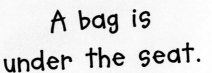

A bag is
on the seat.

Yes? No?

Word Bank

bin

nose

bottle

pond

five **5**

rock

flowers

skunk

four **4**

three **3**

log

two **2**

message

wall